A Sweet New Season

Reflections

DIANNE ROSSOL

 FriesenPress

One Printers Way
Altona, MB R0G 0B0
Canada

www.friesenpress.com

ISBN
978-1-03-916643-1 (Hardcover)
978-1-03-916642-4 (Paperback)
978-1-03-916644-8 (eBook)

1. AGING, WELL-BEING, ACCEPTANCE

Distributed to the trade by The Ingram Book Company

TABLE OF CONTENTS

Preface

The preface for my newest book, *A Sweet New Season: Reflections*, is to continue to reminisce about different situations we all go through and how we can still find joy in the small things. It's not about how much we own because we don't want to be caught up in a materialistic world or competitive way of life. Those things are superficial to what really matters. There will always be people with more than we have and people with less. Happiness is not about having what you want; it's about wanting what you have. Most importantly, we are all better than our circumstances. Furthermore, a person's social status doesn't matter, although some may disagree. What matters is that we, as humans, are social beings, who are always searching to connect with others. What also matters is the vulnerable side that we all have. This vulnerable side is what helps us connect. It's the "human condition" that we all have in common.

We need to be thankful for the things we take for granted because they can be gone in a flash. We are fortunate to live in a civilized society. To put things into perspective, all we have to do is imagine what it would be like to be starving, diseased, and living in squalor. Then we realize just how lucky we are.

Without good health, and a good support network, we have nothing. Living in this world is a privilege. In other words, we were put here for a reason, and that is to make some kind of difference. Each of us is capable of doing something small in a big way. Even something as simple as a smile can do wonders for another person. We must remember, as well, that all of us experience a lack of good judgment from time to time. What I mean is that sometimes we don't think before we act, and we can do or say something that we ordinarily wouldn't. Then we must squirm our way out of the situation or suffer the consequences.

Human frailties are common to each of us.

According to the law of attraction, whatever you send out in the world is what you get back. That theory is evident in John Lennon and Sir Paul McCartney's lyrics for the song "The End" (from the famous, iconic Beatles' *Abbey Road* album). It's about reaching out if we want someone to reach out to us. Simply, we must give in order to receive.

What we will regret in this life (as I have, being a senior) are the chances we never took. A lot of what I write about is learning to trust our intuition. People are not perfect, and we are all on the same path to becoming our best selves, regardless of the challenges we face. Life experience and what we learn about ourselves as we go can be hard lessons, but at the same time the most rewarding of lessons.

With *A Sweet New Season: Reflections*, I feel the need to share what each of us has in common. I want to emphasize that when we look at others, we shouldn't automatically judge them. It is important that we give them the once over, twice. In other words—try and see past the first impression. We are all dealing with something, even if it isn't obvious, and we deserve a second glance. Beauty comes from within.

DIANNE ROSSOL

Dedication

I dedicate this book to the kind, loving, caring souls with HEARTS OF GOLD who "choose" or "adopt" babies or children into their families and give them their forever homes. Love is not biological. There is always room in people's hearts for more love, as well as the ability to nurture.

I also dedicate this book to the many women who sacrifice nine months of their lives and choose to give up their babies in order to give them a better chance at life. It must be the hardest decision in the world to make, and I commend you with heartfelt gratitude.

In both instances, you folks are GIFTS FROM GOD!

PART ONE:
Tributes, Tidings, and Tidbits

To Our Esteemed Doctors and Nurses
(A Tribute)

If it weren't for you *ANGELS OF MERCY*,
We'd all be in serious trouble!
We'd be trapped away inside of our homes,
And living in a fearful, helpless bubble.

You doctors and nurses are exceptional human beings!
Your professional loyalty never waivers!
None of us are exempt from sickness or injury,
So we need you dedicated lifesavers!

You have a calling to want to help people…
And I'm sure there can be much satisfaction in it.
It seems like more than just a job to you.
If it wasn't, you wouldn't be so committed.

Your patience with patients is second to none,
Whether we're well or in misery.
We have faith in you to know what's best for us;
You deserve our deepest respect un-begrudgingly!

You don't go to school all those years for nothing,
And you acquire special skills and expertise.
It takes years to learn what can happen to the body,
And as we age, malfunctions are sure to increase.

We are much in need of **YOU** empathetic souls!
What could happen without you is unthinkable…
If we imagine you not being here for us,
Our lives would be merciless and painful.

It has to be especially challenging
To work in an emergency room situation...
But it must be rewarding when you save someone
After making a split-second decision.

Not everyone can do what you do!
Your jobs depend on a great deal of ability.
You need to be on your toes all the time;
This requires competence and ingenuity!

We want to say **THANK YOU** for everything you do,
And for being the extraordinary people you are!
To all doctors and nurses—the world salutes you!
You are our bright and shining **SUPERSTARS!**

DIANNE ROSSOL

Be Grateful

Go outside and take a good look at what surrounds you…
Smell the smells; see the sights; hear the sounds.
Feel the love you have in your heart,
As you notice the beauty all around.

Be grateful and give thanks to the universe
For what you've been graciously given.
There's no mistake that you are still standing here;
Be thankful to your glorious craftsman!

It will put a smile on your face to think of others…
Like your family and your network of friends.
You are blessing them by giving them a thought or a prayer,
As well as to others on whom you depend.

Be grateful for what you have at the moment.
Don't worry about what you may lack.
Everything you need will come to you in time…
Live for today and try not to look back.

The House That Built You

Think back as far as you can remember…
Of where you come from, and where you've gone since.
Think of the takeaway moments in every instance,
And where you have left your mark or imprint.

Relish those memories and accomplishments,
As fulfillment comes from more than one place.
But there's nothing like the remembrance of home,
That gave you the starting blocks to run your race.

Those roots gave you added strength and confidence—
Not unlike the roots of a mighty oak tree.
Appreciate what you learned from your growing up years
That helped compose your own version of living happily.

As long as you keep your feet on solid ground,
And don't take anything for granted,
No matter where you end up setting down your roots,
You have to bloom where you are planted.

Head in the Clouds

I have spent my life with my head in the clouds—
Not because I am tall or proud, but because I'm a dreamer.
I've imagined great things, more than what I could do or be...
Like having more of a fearless mixture of capabilities.

Somehow I felt I was destined to be isolated or lonely at times.
The dreams that would have once meant the world to me
Never came to pass, but a greater force had the final say.
I find that my life was planned out for me in a different way.

Clarity comes with some of the choices that I make for myself,
Like the friends I select and the self I present for the world
to see.
I know deep down that some of those things I have longed for...
Were never in the cards for me, now or before.

Although miracles happen every day in people's lives,
The cards you are dealt are given for a reason.
Things may not always turn out as you had hoped they would...
But whatever does happen is for your greater good.

Though my head is still up there in the clouds,
I expect it will always be there till the end.
It's a comfort when unexpected blessings come my way,
Even if they come in shapes and ways unimagined.

Start Living

It's not who you are that holds you back;
It's who you think you're not.
It's time for you to start living!
So go out there and give it all you got!

Don't believe everything you think.
Don't let your insecurities stand in the way.
We are all unique with something new to bring.
We've all got something worthwhile to say.

BUT make sure you are not saying *no* to yourself
When you say *yes* to others!
Don't light yourself on fire to keep someone else warm!
Concentrate on yourself and what you hope to discover.

Your mind creates your own reality.
Be that change in the world that you want to see.
Connect with those who have similar interests.
Create your own part of history.

Go get 'em, Champ—go for the gold!
Face down your mental enemies.
Live like there's no tomorrow, but at the same time…
Honour your dreams and life's possibilities!

Voices from the Past

People come and go in our lives;
Some stay or move on, for whatever reason.
Others need something different from a friendship;
Reasons can be obvious or unspoken.

Positive encounters come with most;
Those that aren't, weren't meant to be.
We learn something about ourselves from each relationship,
And with each there are always peaks and valleys.

Later in life we remember with fondness...
The good times we had, more than the reverse.
Those times brought us to where we are now,
And bad times, from the past, are no longer a curse.

Voices from the past may haunt us...
In both good and in not-such-good ways,
But we have to think of it like this:
Each of those voices shaped us into who we are today.

The Soldier in the Khaki Tuxedo

We salute our men and women in the khaki tuxedos—
Who stand tall for you and me!
Whether they're at home or on the battlefield...
They're the reason we are free.

It's not just a job; it's a solemn declaration...
To honour and protect their fellow man!
They're committed to their families and country,
As only gallant guardian soldiers can!

We must take care of these brave protectors!
They see things nobody should have to see!
They are heroic in every sense of the word,
And deserve to be supported, at home, subsequently!

They could come back with PTSD or injuries—
And need our assistance as they convalesce.
They need to be cared for like any hero,
And not have any additional stress!

To the men and women in the armed forces—
Valiant defenders of our freedom...
We **THANK YOU** sincerely for your service!
You make us proud to sing our national anthem!

DIANNE ROSSOL

Be Mindful of What You Say

When your head tells you NOT to say something
But then you blurt it out anyway—
You could be at the very end of your tether,
And not care at that point what you say.

There are instances where you may be self-doubting.
People, who don't know you, may take you seriously.
It's that first impression others might hold on to...
Then you'll need to prove yourself otherwise, constantly.

The law of attraction says you attract what you fear...
That is usually criticism, condemnation, or judgement.
Self-esteem plays a huge role in how you communicate.
So don't utter something about yourself that you shouldn't!

Trust your sixth sense; it's your gut trying to warn you.
To think before you speak is a valuable tool.
Although it's so easy to just be impulsive and blurt—
Try and hold back so you don't sound like a fool.

People take you at your own sense of self-worth...
So be careful not to demean your own character!
Some can and will play on your insecurities—
Your words might come back and haunt you thereafter.

Who We Are

No matter our beliefs…
Or which country we are from,
We are all God's children,
Each and every one!

There is only one God,
As earth has one moon and one sun.
We live under the same roof.
We are under one heaven.

In His eyes we're all one shade…
The colour of promise and love!
We were sent here for a reason—
And masterfully designed from above.

We breathe the same air,
Cry the same tears,
Smile the same smile,
Feel the same fears.

We are all God's children!
We're just trying to make our way…
And survive in a world of differences,
On any given day.

Though this is not an easy world
We have the same basic needs…
To live a life without hardship,
In a safe place where we are free!

DIANNE ROSSOL

We want to maintain our dignity...
And work to support ourselves,
Contribute to society,
And in turn—help someone else.

It is our civic duty, as decent people—
To care for our fellow human beings...
To give a damn and help if we can,
With whatever it is that they need.

Having Faith

Wildlife and birds share the earth with us…
Like us, they're out there trying to survive.
They, too, will do anything to protect themselves
In the habitats in which they thrive.

Their instincts rely on what is seen and not seen;
They intuitively know what to gravitate to.
They have some kind of built-in radar,
That miraculously allows them to make do.

Birds and wildlife speak their own language;
They adapt to the surroundings they are in.
Resources are out there to live abundant lives.
That's what wildlife and humans have in common.

All we need is faith in what is seen and unseen!
Our trust in the universe is essential to our needs.
So long as our faith doesn't waver in bad times…
Our great God above will indeed intercede.

We can't buy our way to heaven,
But we can earn it with our faith and conviction.
We need to trust that God will look after us—
He's the Master of all creation!

DIANNE ROSSOL

We All Desire to Be Seen

It has nothing to do with ego,
Although each of us has one of those.
It is part of our makeup to want to be seen;
We also want to be listened to,
And to have our say and find our place.
No matter what type of personality we have...
It's all a part of our design as human beings.

Your ego has to do with your false self,
Whereas wanting to be seen is natural.
It has everything to do with our identities.
It's about being transparent about who we are...
Our traits, our character, and our qualities,
Without any pretentiousness...
It's about being able to share our personal stories.

Every Night Is Friday Night!

Retirement means working at living not living at work.
Just think about all the discounts you get as a senior...
It is the world's longest, well-deserved coffee break.
Just think of all the new friends you will make.

It means being on permanent vacation—*IMAGINE!*
Retirement means you now have nothing but time...
You can do everything you always wanted to do:
Take a course, go on a trip, or construct something new.

Every day has an open *happy hour* invitation.
Enjoy those potlucks and bring your own lawn chair.
While away the hours by telling a bunch of tall tales.
It's time for you to blaze yourself a new trail.

The only thing about doing nothing
Is that you never know when you are finished.
Now you can look forward to weekdays with delight
Best of all—cheers! Every night is Friday night!

Fall

The air is crisp, the birds are gone.
Leaves rustle under your feet.
The days are shorter; the mood changes...
A cool retreat from the summer heat.

There's a feeling of calmness in the air...
You might enjoy a scenic hayride,
As you feel the glow from the harvest moon,
When summer and fall collide.

There is plenty of pumpkin and pecan pie;
Then there are pumpkin spice lattes.
Snuggle around the fire pit with a blanket,
And watch the fire blaze.

We celebrate fall with Thanksgiving...
And reflect on what that means.
It is to reap what we sow then sleep to renew,
With the emergence of wintergreen.

We All Long to Be Somebody's Kid

We all have that need for parental nurturing
No matter how old we happen to be.
That guiding light on my shoulder...
Gave me reassurance and security.
I still want to curl up on my dad's knee.

Nothing can ever take the place of those times!
Then we become the knee our own kids adhere to.
We think back to the time when we were kids...
We all needed that bounce or hug as we grew,
And when our moms and dads came to the rescue.

Now in this muddled up adult world we live in...
We wish we could revert to those days.
Stories read to us were like a warm blanket,
And *sleep tight* was a comforting phrase.
Things seemed right with the world in all ways.

DIANNE ROSSOL

Gingerbread Wishes and Lollipop Dreams

Can't wait to meet you face to face
So we can see the wonder in your eyes.
May all your thoughts and dreams be sweet!
We'll be there to soothe your cries.
May you always remember
The love we have for you!
May God carry you the distance,
And may all your dreams come true!

When they told us you were coming—
We felt a joy we'd never known!
You are our little miracle;
Can't wait till you are born!
You are such a blessing,
That we've been in love with for so long!
This is what we hope for you
As we sing your welcome song…

Gingerbread wishes and lollipop dreams,
Kaleidoscopes and jelly beans,
Lullabies and jingle bells,
Carousels and wishing wells,
Magic wands and Peter Pan,
Donald Duck and Disneyland,
Angels to watch over you at night…
And keep you safe till morning light.

Harry Potter and the Wizard of Oz,
The Easter Bunny and Santa Claus,
Pixies, elves, and nursery rhymes,
Unicorns, ice cream, and story times,
Ten tiny fingers and ten tiny toes...
May love follow you wherever you go.
We wish you stardust, rainbows, and bright sunbeams...
And gingerbread wishes and lollipop dreams!

Hiding in Plain Sight

When you are looking at the answer
That is hiding in plain sight—
You might have to try and convince yourself
To do the thing that feels right.

You know in your heart of hearts
That although it's the right thing to do…
Others may still not approve but
You've got to do what's right for you!

Don't do things just to please others,
Even if you have a different point of view.
What works for you may not work for them;
Trust your own internal queue.

There are no instructions that come with life
But you need to trust your intuition!
If the answer is as clear as the nose on your face,
Then trust your own cognition.

Call to Duty

When someone out there needs some help,
We do what we can—when we can.
Whether it is a hand out or a hand up...
Being here for each other is part of God's plan!

Put yourself in the other person's shoes;
We all need to reach out now and then.
It only makes sense that if you feel that pang—
Imagine yourself in that same situation.

It's hard to see someone suffer
Through any kind of negative event!
Sharing with someone who is trustworthy...
Will be supportive and time well spent.

We are supposed to have each other's backs,
No matter what the circumstances may be...
Whether a traumatic experience has taken place,
Or something of a different uncertainty!

DIANNE ROSSOL

Thank You!
(A Tribute to Mom and Dad)

For all of those ice cream cones
I dribbled down my chin...
For dreams come true, and memories
I cling to deep within...

For giving me the breath of life
So helpless at three weeks,
For gracing me with unwavering love
That we all deserve and seek...

For your unselfish acts of kindness,
For your unconditional care,
For giving so much of yourselves,
I could have ended up elsewhere...

For everything you've done for me
Mere words cannot repay;
I thank you for the sacrifices
You made each and every day!

For all the values I have learned
From you, my precious mom and dad—
To set out in this busy world
With the training I have had...

For your decision to choose me,
And bring me up with love,
It was God who sent you to me
Through an angel from above!

When I was born into this world
And could have made the choice...
I would have searched the world throughout
Until YOU heard my voice!

For all that you have blessed on me
Throughout the passing years,
I'll hold them tightly in my heart
As cherished souvenirs!

A Sweet New Season

Part of life is what we create for ourselves,
As well as for the benefit of others.
It's not like the four seasons that already exist;
It's our own new seasons that we discover!

It's how we live our lives between the intervals of:
Being a kid, a teen, an adult, and a senior.
We grow as we go and develop wisdom along the way.
Each new season has a common factor...

We look to our mentors as well as to others,
And we strengthen those bonds as we grow.
By the time we become seniors, though we're still learning,
We find we are no longer the selves we used to know.

Our ideas and ideals change along the way.
Each new season has its own revelations.
There is always something new to uncover...
Life's train stops at every station.

In childhood we depend on our guardians;
In adolescence we go to school for instruction;
In adulthood we establish our paths going forward;
As seniors we appreciate our own identification.

It takes a lifetime to know where we're going...
And a lot of reflection to know where we've been!
We learn to navigate the twists and turns as we go,
With each sweet new season we find ourselves in.

Life Is One Big Question Mark (?)

Life is full of unfinished sentences…
And unanswered questions:
What? When? Why? Who? How? Where?
We spend our lives looking for answers—
Sometimes they just aren't there!

We can't live our lives with remorse.
Tell the people you love, that you love them!
Don't regretfully leave anything unsaid…
And no matter how hard it is to say those words—
There is nothing at all to dread!

We are grateful for the answers we do get.
But where we've come from and where we're going…
Only heaven knows—
So those unanswered questions will remain…
And that's just how life rolls!

DIANNE ROSSOL

Christmas Joy and Tiny Treasures

Handmade decorations
Mom created just for me…
With stitch and bead and bobble,
To adorn my Christmas tree;

Precious, bright, and sparkling,
Sweet treasures from her heart…
Her love for me continues…
Now that we're apart.

Candy canes and popcorn chains,
Beads and bells and balls,
Garlands strung and stockings hung…
Angels, stars, and dolls;

Manger scene and a tree so green…
God and gifts and glee…
Carols sung and church bells rung…
Praise and glory be!

Blessed by an Angel

You'll know it if you've found an angel
That looks out for you and your well-being.
Sometimes they are invisible,
And oftentimes they're plainly seen.

When you've been blessed beyond comprehension…
You can feel it, so you can tell.
It's almost like you've experienced a miracle!
It's like someone cast a magic spell.

You'll know the next time an angel blesses you…
It may be unseen or in human disguise.
At times when you least expect it or have given up hope—
That angel has heard your silent, burdened cries!

When you are at a crossroads of doubt and fear…
And are having an emotional tug-of-war,
Sometimes you'll be blessed with some miracle…
By someone who is a real-life avatar!

DIANNE ROSSOL

Doctors of the Mind
(A Tribute)

You are specialists who deserve to be praised!
You see us at our absolute worst,
And when we are having better days...
After we feel we've been damned or cursed.

You take our problems and help turn them around.
You lift us up to the sunny side...
When we are feeling upside down,
You are our gentle wellness guides.

You tell us to forget the past—it's over; it's gone!
There's still time to achieve great things...
So we can hold our heads up and carry on,
While better equipped for whatever life brings.

You rebuild broken lives and give people hope.
You are experts and love what you do!
You prescribe appropriate ways for us to cope,
And help us see things from a different view.

You recognize the potential in everyone
No matter what cards we have been dealt...
So we can get back to living and have fun,
Despite how out of control we have felt!

You know how to bring out the best in us.
You help revive our sense of self-worth.
If, in you, we keep our patience, faith, and trust—
It would be like witnessing our own rebirth!

You remind us to make the best of each day,
And to live each one to the fullest (for instance).
We never know what might come our way...
But we can move forward with more resilience.

Not to pay tribute to you wouldn't seem right.
You inspire us to become our best selves!
We know things don't happen overnight...
But are certain we've got the right help!

You are all a blessing to everyone!
To say **THANK YOU** doesn't seem enough...
YOU are **EXCEPTIONAL**—in my opinion.
You give us new hope after things have been tough!

DIANNE ROSSOL

Banff, Alberta, My Happy Place

If you want to see the most awe-inspiring place on earth,
Hop on a plane from wherever you live…
Travel to the picturesque Rocky Mountains in Alberta, Canada.
You'll never see anything more impressive!

In and around breathtaking Banff and Lake Louise,
You'll find the most jaw-dropping scenery!
Not to mention—it's a photographer's paradise,
And a place of unsurpassed beauty!

If you are into hiking, world-class golf, and alpine skiing—
This place would satisfy your wish list.
You'll never see glacial lakes of a more turquoise blue!
You may be drawn there to canoe or fish.

You'll be enchanted by cascading waterfalls!
You might want to heighten your senses on a gondola ride—
Up to the top of Sulphur Mountain, where…
The landscape will leave you breathless and wide-eyed!

Nestled in the magnificent heart of the Bow Valley
Is the luxurious Fairmont Banff Springs Hotel!
It is sometimes referred to as a "Scottish Baronial Castle."
This is the only way to describe it in a nutshell.

If there was ever a destination *HAPPY PLACE*, Banff is it—
Not to mention the picture-perfect Lake Louise!
Sight-seeing, wildlife, and the crisp mountain air…
And multiple activities are sure to please!

The Rockies are bustling with aliveness!
That includes an array of wildlife like mountain goats,
Elk, bighorn sheep, grizzly bears and the like…
Everything the park pamphlets denote.

It doesn't matter what time of year it is,
The area is full of adventure!
You might even want to try white water rafting—
An exhilarating activity for the thrill-seeker!

Banff is a world-wide tourist destination!
It has been kept pristine in every sense of the word.
It's a place of charming, unrivalled beauty…
That lives up to everything you have read or heard!

Everyone Has Their Own Idea of Shangri-la

Whether it's skiing in the snow-capped Swiss Alps,
Or snowshoeing outdoors in Alaska…
It could be a swim in an aquarium with dolphins;
What is your Shangri-la—I ask ya?

Is it the thrill of a library full of books to read?
Or could it be spending time in scenic Banff, Alberta?
Or salmon fishing off the coast of British Columbia?
Or sipping a Mai Tai on a beach in Antigua?

It could be precious alone time with the one you love.
It could be unwinding in a nice hot shower.
It could be sitting in a peaceful garden…
Watching the butterflies, and smelling the flowers.

It could be taking a big trip you've been saving for,
Or enjoying a buffet in a fine restaurant.
It could be receiving support from loved ones,
While being awarded for an achievement!

It could be reaping the rewards of a healthy lifestyle…
Or (in general) long-awaited dreams come true.
It could be the rekindling of an old friendship,
Or realizing the meaning of your own value!

It could be excelling at something you love—
Like a sport, or any volunteer efforts.
It could be a skill or appreciation of some kind of art,
Or even the thrill of attending concerts.

This kind of puts things into perspective—
To realize just how lucky we are…
To even have a Shangri-la to dream about,
In a secure place of freedom not war.

Tidbits

People throw you tidbits and sometimes a bone;
They'll taunt you with a game of cat and mouse.
They'll tease you a bit, and then have mercy on you;
You'll soon find out who's a friend or a louse.

The more you tell others, the more ammo they get…
To seek out your Achilles heel!
Some will use information to get a rise out of you…
Or see how much more you'll reveal.

There are those who will use things against you,
So they can puff up their own self-esteem!
They make you feel bad for the way you are;
Those people are self-inflating and mean!

Beware of those who play with your emotions…
And try to make you look like a fool!
They stomp on your sense of self-worth—
This is a form of covert ridicule!

Time Flies, You Are the Pilot

Make the most of each and every day!
Time flies and you are the pilot...
If there is something interesting new to try—
Then by all means go out and try it!

All of a sudden, ten years go by...
There are unfulfilled dreams waiting for you!
You'd better get after those dreams right now!
Your clock is telling you you've got lots left to do!

Time has a way of escaping, especially when
We put off what we could do till tomorrow.
You are the pilot of your own destiny!
REMEMBER: Time—you can't steal back or borrow!

DIANNE ROSSOL

Talk About Relief!

It's such a relief to make a decision,
After wavering for years!
Should I or shouldn't I continue with this?
One minute it's smiles, then the next it's tears...

Simply—if there are more tears than smiles,
The answer is staring us in the face!
It's time to move on and move forward.
Our attentions belong in a different place.

No One is Born Perfect

We all come out naked and unknowing,
Of the life we are about to live.
The truth of it is—we learn by our mistakes,
And the circumstances we learn to live with.

With understanding we can move on ahead.
With vulnerability we learn to connect.
With the pieces of each intricate puzzle—
We become our own life architect.

We build perspective and find purpose.
We develop our own attitude.
We navigate by the things we are capable of,
And with the knowledge we have accrued.

The curveballs that are thrown at us in life…
Take us into another dimension.
It's not as simple as "live and let live,"
But to stay positive when there is dissention.

We learn to find joy in the little things—
Not the yacht or the penthouse suite.
It's in the time we spend with the ones we love…
At the same table where we have a seat!

We live and learn and grow as we go,
To become our best version, personally.
We were NOT put on this earth to be perfect—
But to offer a uniquely different personality.

DIANNE ROSSOL

Your Conscience

Trust the little man on your shoulder,
When something is gnawing at your craw!
If it's just a fleeting thought, then let it go;
But if it keeps up—listen intently;
It's a sign to act on the vision you heard or saw.

The little man on your shoulder is your conscience,
Or it could be a signal from overhead.
Listen to the little man—he speaks loudly.
Proceed even if you don't know why…
Deny any reservations and listen to him instead!

Trust your conscience, not your imagination!
Your inner voice is trying to alert you to act.
Your gut will, at the same time, give you a hint,
And although you may not know why—
Listen, follow through, and don't retract!

It's a Diverse World Out There

There are those who are willing;
There are those who are not.
There are those who teach,
And those who don't want to be taught!

Then there are the rednecks,
As well as those who follow the rules.
Then there are those who are self-entitled—
They are the chumps and the fools!

There are self-serving people;
Then there are the ones who give.
There are those who are cautious,
And those who are impulsive.

Everyone has something to offer
From humanity's bag of tricks.
The world is a kaleidoscope...
Each montage has a different matrix!

There is justice and injustice—
Each with its own circumstance!
It's how we react to either,
That helps us decide on how to take a stance.

Issues, rules, and constitutional rights,
Affect our own theories and notions.
How we conduct ourselves in this world,
Will depend on our beliefs and devotions.

DIANNE ROSSOL

Then there are those without a conscience;
They have no regard for their fellow man.
Some are only out for themselves,
And of others they don't give a damn!

They will have to wrestle with their demons—
As we all have to do now and then.
But most people do care for others!
They are most women and men.

Baby Steps

"Put one foot in front of the other,"
And "It's one day at a time," they say
I mean, there really are no other choices...
As to how we live each day!

Sure, there are unplanned instances,
That we must try to navigate.
Everything is a process that takes time...
A lot depends on the choices we make!

We need to have goals and direction.
We need a good plan in place.
We need something to look forward to.
With these things—we set our own pace.

Not often things just fall into our laps.
Not often we can do things alone.
But whatever we end up doing...
It's the baby steps that get it done!

DIANNE ROSSOL

Mother Nature and Father Time

We picture Father Time as an old man with a beard,
And Mother Nature as our earth, and its weather.
Perhaps they intermingle as the earth and the sky—
But they are definitely linked together!

Father Time depicts power and leadership.
Mother Nature is our nurturer and sustainer.
She nourishes and provides what we need to survive.
Father Time is our overseer and controller.

Mother Nature symbolizes climate, and nutrition,
While Father Time sets the terms and limits.
Everything on earth is given a reason and a season.
Father Time is the keeper of all secrets.

While Father Time allows, Mother Nature endures—
Both are endless and immortal!
And both, together, are our directors…
They control everything on earth as a whole!

Road Rash and Wrinkles

Mirror, mirror, on the—uh—floor...
Time just didn't fly by—it soared!
Who the hell is this I see?
I need a yearbook so I can recognize me!

Did I accomplish as much as I had hoped?
Has my life been a colourful kaleidoscope?
Or is it a quilt of dreams that came to pass?
Who is this I see in the mirror—alas?

Have I faced my life with limitations?
Did I look at myself with apprehension?
Did I hold back due to some kind of fear?
Where the years have gone, seems so unclear!

Why are there lapses in my memory?
Some of the things I recall are a bit blurry!
All of a sudden twenty years whooshed by—
I wish I'd kept a diary—to help clarify!

There are more days gone than in front of me.
I want to embrace the future in harmony.
What matters most, is that I've loved and lived,
And still have so much more to give.

Now as I look at others who are at this stage—
I see what truly matters at this golden age.
The road rash and wrinkles have been well-earned,
But they're really of no consequence or concern.

DIANNE ROSSOL

The Clock Is Always Ticking

We wish time would stop to capture precious moments…
Or to honour those we have lost!
Tick-tock, tick-tock, not going to stop…
Your watch could quit working, but time still carries on!
Tick-tock, tick-tock, time will not stand still…
If it did, a person would always remain the same age;
A butterfly would still be resting on a flower;
Whatever season you are in, the air would be lifeless;
The birds would quit singing and your food would quit cooking.
Water would stop running and there'd be no ocean tides.
All living things would be frozen still in time—
Like when you pause a movie to take a break.

Pain would be unbearable, if time took its time!
People's brains would stop functioning…
Imagine the world stopping in mid-sentence?
People would disintegrate into what was once air…
And become single molecules floating freely in nothingness—
Like there was never a world in the first place!
Tick-tock, tick-tock, be glad time does not stand still!
Time has a mysterious kindness:
It gives us back memories and love that were lost.
The clock is always ticking, *tick-tock, tick-tock*…
Good thing time does not stand still…
(THINK) No one would get paid if they weren't *on the clock!*

Past, Present, and Future

The *PAST* has passed, **LET IT GO!**
Forget about the mistakes you made.
Dismiss others' indiscretions against you;
Those prices have already been paid.

Let go of any guilt or shame!
We all feel guilt from wrongdoing at times.
If we don't let go, those instances will eat us alive.
Know that each of us has these hills to climb.

The *PRESENT* means **LIVE FOR TODAY!**
For you never know what tomorrow may see.
Can't worry about tomorrow either…
So make today the best it can be!

Go to bed each night with a grateful heart.
Any worries can wait until tomorrow.
Before bed write a list of things bothering you;
Unclutter your mind on paper—just let it flow.

The *FUTURE* is out of our control.
We navigate each day as it arises.
Our days are full of pluses and minuses,
And sometimes pleasant surprises!

A brilliant future is based on a forgotten past…
All we really have is today.
We can't think too far ahead,
But for sure, we can't keep tripping over yesterday!

DIANNE ROSSOL

Comfort and Joy

Comfort is a cozy blanket and a glass of wine,
A crackling fire in the fireplace,
A good book to read on a rainy day,
While being entranced in its warm embrace...

Being stuck inside in a snowstorm,
With family gathered round—
Conversation, hot chocolate, and cozy beds...
All under the same roof, safe and sound.

At Christmas we forget our problems,
As we celebrate comfort and joy.
We hang our stockings and decorate the tree,
As the kiddies dream of that new toy!

There is delight around every corner,
If we step back from the hustle and bustle.
We enjoy the peace we can create for ourselves,
If we take our foot off the throttle!

Reflections

After thinking back on my childhood,
And how much more secure things seemed...
It was a time when we weren't afraid of anything!
With stars in our eyes, we dreamed big dreams!

Our parents were our safety nets,
When things ever went awry!
We could always go to them without fear,
And hugs and kisses were in good supply.

Organized sports were always on the agenda,
Just as much as they are here and now.
Lots of time, as well, for self-interest courses...
You'd pack as much in, as time would allow.

On Sunday, all the stores were closed
In reverence of God's day of rest!
There were no such things as walk-in clinics.
And when you saw your doctor, you got an hour at best.

We weren't allowed to wear slacks to school;
We had to change into a skirt or dress.
Rules finally changed in that regard;
Back in the late sixties—they called it PROGRESS!

We spent lots of time outside playing.
There were conversations at the dinner table.
There were no computers or cell phones,
Nor was there any TV cable.

DIANNE ROSSOL

Neighbours watched out for each other's kids.
The adults congregated on weekends.
Kids played in each other's backyards,
Or at the playground where they met up with their friends.

The only infraction was that we raided gardens,
For peas and carrots and the like...
Sometimes we got caught and other times we didn't;
We'd just take off on our bikes.

Our neighbours were addressed as Mr. or Mrs.;
We were taught manners until we were blue.
There was no swearing, talking back... only respect.
We were taught gratitude with a PLEASE and THANK YOU!

In the 60s and 70s we had no air conditioning;
It was uncommon where we lived in those days.
Environmental issues were not a concern yet—
Like air pollution, and contaminated waterways.

We could hardly wait till our school days were over!
We wanted to grow up too fast as it was.
It wasn't as easy as we imagined, being out on our own.
So growing up too fast had its flaws.

Childhood responsibilities seemed far less,
After we graduated from high school.
When it came time to make more serious decisions...
Those childhood obligations seemed minuscule.

Each era has its strengths and drawbacks.
It's hard to keep up with fast-paced technology.
Now there's the added burden of climate change!
There needs to be more awareness and accountability!

The Memories Get Louder

As memories come back from time to time,
They get louder and become more profound!
You can't undo or change the past—good or bad;
You need to get off that merry-go-round!

Nothing you could have done would have changed things,
Though your thoughts might contradict that belief!
Don't beat yourself up—what is done is done!
You are just causing yourself undue grief!

Nobody ever said life was fair!
We are all victims at one time or another.
Life is about us being on a learning curve.
Sometimes we're the loser and sometimes the winner.

The memories of the people you've lost
Whether they are still alive or dead,
Get louder when you think of what could have been…
Get those notions out of your head.

You can't continue to mourn what wasn't meant to be,
Even though you wish otherwise!
Keep the memories but keep them real—
Or you'll continue to agonize.

The idea is to make every day count.
Do something for others and then for you too.
Let the memories out of your bank for a while…
But don't let them yell at you!

DIANNE ROSSOL

Authenticity Is Everything!

Be real; tell your story; be proud of it!
There are people out there just like you.
They think and feel the same way as you do.
Never doubt your moral virtue.

Remember that whoever you perceive yourself to be…
You are and never will be alone!
There are those who have the same set of values.
You weren't born to be floundering on your own.

Don't sacrifice yourself for the sake of others.
Live your life authentically, just as you are!
It is **EVERYTHING** to be true to who you were born to be—
Staying transparent will take you far.

Not everyone will like you no matter what!
Some will, some won't, and some won't care.
But stick with those who have common traits and ideals;
This will help take care of our own welfare!

Not Everything Can Be Forgiven

I don't know who those people are
Who can forgive and then forget!
I am not one of those people, unfortunately,
And that is not a great characteristic or epithet.

Although I have trouble letting go,
I know I can't move forward unless I forgive…
Especially if someone hurts me on purpose—
Then, of course, it is truly offensive!

How do you forgive a nasty neighbour?
Do you have to move to get away?
Sometimes reason and compromise don't work!
It's either leave or put-up and stay.

It's much easier to forgive someone
If an apology and a hug are involved.
We all say things off the cuff sometimes—
But if we catch ourselves, hopefully it will get resolved.

How do you forgive murder?
You hear of this on the news all day long!
What are assault weapons doing in a civilized society?
Most people want to see them gone!!!

Since money is the root of all evil,
Some people think they outclass those who struggle.
Gotta have, gotta get, gotta be better than, gotta win—
It is phony and superficial.

DIANNE ROSSOL

If you are honest about your own parameters...
I'm sure your ability to forgive has its limits!
We are only human and have our breaking points,
But standing firm on our beliefs has its merits.

Morality

Our first impulse when evil strikes
Is shock—then anger—then grief!
How could anyone use people as targets?
It leaves us horrified in disbelief.

We like to think that people are civilized
And come from a place of compassion.
But some people are like wolves; there's strength in packs;
They can become merciless and brazen!

There seems to be a lack of shame or guilt out there;
Some people snap and become deranged!
Until they revise laws with more severe consequences,
We'll never see acts of violence change.

When something of this magnitude happens...
Compassionate people DO emerge on the scene.
They come out of the woodwork everywhere,
When horrendous things happen that are unforeseen!

Fortunately, there is more good in the world than evil—
Although the news, these days, suggests otherwise!
Evil may breed evil, but good also breeds good.
Samaritans come to the rescue of the victimized.

Makes us wonder if good will indeed prevail
In a world that is divided so adamantly—
When violence is on the rise everywhere it seems...
What has happened to the voice of morality?

DIANNE ROSSOL

Secrets and Lies

Don't tell people anything you don't want repeated,
Unless it's a trusted family member or close friend.
Secrets don't stay secrets for very long otherwise.
They spread faster than you can comprehend!

Now, lies will come back and bite you!
If you think they can't, you are lying to yourself as well!
You might even start believing your own lies—
Then when you are confronted, you'll feel like hell.

It's easy to tell if someone is lying to you,
Especially if it's face to face!
If they can't look you in the eye or are fidgety—
It's a good indicator that this is the case.

Both lies and secrets are deceptive;
They can lead to isolation and mistrust.
You are only as sick as your secrets and lies!
So being able to unload them is a definite must.

Mistakes Are Made in Haste

Don't make decisions based on lack of information.
Snap decisions can lead to trouble—
Unlike in emergency room situations (for example),
Where decisions are made on the double!

Most mistakes, made in haste, carry penalties.
Accuracy is always better than speed.
So don't hit the buzzer too quickly—
You'll have a better chance to succeed!

Although mistakes are common to each of us,
Once-in-a-blue-moon things may work in reverse.
But it's best to take time to contemplate…
And don't answer before you think first!

DIANNE ROSSOL

Old and Familiar

There's no friend like an old friend,
And there are no soles like worn out shoes.
Then there's that comfy sweater with holes in it—
That helps us cozy away the blues.

All take us back to once upon a time…
Just like a song on the radio,
Or an old movie or TV show—
Flashbacks to pieces of the past we used to know.

All these comforts from our pasts,
Like candles with a certain scent—
Remind us of people, places, or things,
And specific times that were happily spent!

Scents are powerful reminders…
Like the smell of your mom's perfume,
Or the aftershave your dad splashed on.
It's as if they are standing there in the room.

An old friend takes us even further,
Through that time capsule as we reminisce.
Memories we had stored away are recalled…
With sentimental bliss!

Familiar places are another special sign
Of things that happened way back when.
Like your old house and your old neighbourhood—
They stir up those good endorphins again.

It's funny how we seem to remember...
The good times more than the bad!
Our senses intensify as we recall memories...
That take us back to the good times we had.

To Tantalize Your Senses

Fresh coffee brewing
Turkey stuffing
Popcorn popping
Fresh bread
Cinnamon buns
Bacon frying
Roast beef and gravy
Hot rum toddy
Vanilla
Rosemary chicken
The scent of pine...

Puppy kisses
A warm, crackling fire
A soothing voice
Nostalgic music
Flickering candlelight
A haloed moon
Christmas morning
Laughter
The smell of new car leather
The first snow fall
Orange potpourri...

Love songs
A good book
A friendly glance
A bubble bath
A shooting star
Crisp mountain air

Morning dew
A compliment
Spring flowers
A gentle rain
Fresh cut grass...

Spotting an owl
Cuddly kittens
Giggling babies
An "I Love You"
A kind word
Doing for others
A warm blanket
An old photograph
Home movies
Butterflies
A smile...

The Joy of Living Is Giving

It could be something as little as a smile
That could lighten someone's load.
It could be buying the next person in line a coffee.
It will surely make your own heart overflow.

If you give, you get more out of it
Than the recipient you gave something to.
Compliment those who serve you with gratitude,
No matter what profession they are into.

Give what you can spare to the food bank…
Or help the person short of change at the cashier.
Stop to see if someone is okay if they're struggling.
It will offer them a wee bit of comfort or cheer.

It doesn't take money to be a Good Samaritan.
You could volunteer and offer your assistance…
At a place for the challenged or disabled.
No one will turn you away with any resistance.

You could be a Secret Santa
If you want to help a family in need.
Or you could spend some time with a lonely old soul.
Either way you will have done a good deed.

Do things out of the goodness of your heart…
Not because someone tells you to.
It's whatever you feel comfortable doing—
Any good deed will come back to bless you!

The joy of living is giving…
So long as it's straight from the heart!
One small gesture goes a long, long way;
In the grand scheme, you are doing your part!

Only God Knows Our Longings

With the yearnings that are plaguing us,
God knows, in our hearts, what we're feeling.
And the things that are usually challenging to us—
He knows what's important to our well-being.

When those deep unspoken longings mean a lot,
And have been preying on our hearts for a while...
Some kind of remedy might show up out of nowhere;
We'll sense it is God working in His *mysterious* style.

Sometimes we don't even have to pray out loud.
God still finds a way to put our troubles at rest.
This may come unexpectedly, in ways we never dreamed;
Then we'll believe we've been truly blessed!

When we feel we aren't worthy of God's blessings,
His intervention will let us know He's still there.
Then we'll realize we're not alone in our struggles,
And that we are always in His divine loving care.

An Ode to Our Paw Pals

I can't wait to meet my fur babies in heaven!
There'll be a special place and time to reunite.
They will now stay young and healthy forever.
Without them, heaven just wouldn't seem right!

Can you imagine that long-awaited reunion?
After mourning our losses all those years…
Heaven is a place of unconditional love, after all!
There will be spinning tails and snuggles and happy tears!

Our fur babies bring so much joy to our lives!
I look forward to seeing them on the other side…
Along with our other cherished loved ones.
We will be truly smitten, joyful, and teary-eyed!

We will play and laugh and sing and dance,
As our paw pals frolic in heaven's playground!
There will be hugs and kisses in abundance;
In the place where pure love, peace, and glory abound!

DIANNE ROSSOL

Whispering Winds

As whispering winds speak graciously...
We hear murmurs of loved ones now passed.
The seasons flow as they interchange,
And those whispers speak with a loving caress.

They remind us of bygone eras—
With sighs of love and life and loss.
They speak of old and friendly faces.
We might even hear the voice of God.

If we take the time to listen
To gentle breezes from time to time—
A tender voice might pop into our head;
It may be elevated or sublime.

As the sands of time reveal themselves...
The winds' whispers come and go too.
If we listen to them now and again—
Lost voices may surprise us out of the blue.

To Fill a House With Love

It takes caring supportive people
To fill a house with unconditional love.
Though people may have differences,
It doesn't have to be push and shove.

Caring for one another—
Is something close-knit families do!
It is about having each other's backs…
Despite any opposing points of view.

We are all just people with opinions,
Whether they be right or wrong.
Family is family no matter what…
Even if we don't sing the same song.

At the end of the day, we show up,
No matter what it is that brings us together.
That's what it takes to fill a house with love—
In either pleasant or stormy weather.

DIANNE ROSSOL

Snowmen Fall to Earth Unassembled

Snowmen fall to earth unassembled,
Like diamonds in the rough.
Fragmented and undeveloped—
Flakes are laying there like fluff.

Snowmen are unperfected
Until someone shapes them into rolls.
Otherwise, they'll stay formless and incomplete,
Like sculptures without souls.

Though lifeless while under construction,
They are still in the making, and raw.
They need eyes, a nose, a pipe, and a scarf…
With props to help finish the glistening jigsaw.

As snowmen fall to earth unassembled,
And we see their souls come into being—
We enjoy the character kiddies give them,
Until they thaw away in spring.

PART TWO:
Trials and Coming to Terms

They Would Want You to Carry On

After accepting the passing of the people you love,
Know—you'll eventually meet again.
When it's your time, you are going to where they are,
Though it's not up to you as to when.

Looking forward to seeing them again
Can be something you can hold tightly to.
In the meantime, live every day as if it's your last.
You've still got more living to do!

Loved ones will be waiting on the other side
With open arms to welcome you there—
But until then you need to carry on in their light…
They'd want what is best for your health and welfare.

There will be a heavenly reunion like no other!
No more yearning, no more tears, or misery.
You'll be free of all earthly struggles;
There will be no hardship, worries, or anxiety.

Carry on with what your loved ones would wish for you.
Wear their badge of honour as they watch from above.
It may seem like a lot to live up to, but recognize…
That you were, and still are, unconditionally loved!

I Hope You Remember

You are my precious kids and I hope you think of me,
And the things we did together (once) as a happy family.
There were many good times and I hope you agree.
I know I'm not perfect, but I hope you remember me...

There are two sides to every story, and I see you went with one.
I waited until you both grew up before I chose to run.
It wasn't you who I was leaving, but the time had finally come.
Sorry you haven't heard my side and chose to go with one...

Some day you will remember—all the good times that we had.
You may have pulled the plug on me, but I am still your dad!
In my heart—you are a huge part of my life and I'm SO glad.
I was with you for a while at least, but I miss the times we had.

If you could only hear my side; you are old enough to see...
Why I had to leave as life is short so I, too, could be happy.
It wasn't working with your mother, and I needed to be free!
If you'll take a close look back, you will understand—you'll see!

Please know my heart is with both of you, each and every day.
Don't you think I've paid the price to give your mom her way?
I feel hopelessly abandoned by you, is all that I can say!
You'll always own a huge piece of my heart—forever plus a day!

Some day you'll lose someone precious; then you'll understand...
What I've been going through all these years, without you—if
you can.
I didn't think you'd desert me; it wasn't in the plan!
I truly wish the best for you, but really hoped you'd understand!

DIANNE ROSSOL

As you choose to carry the burden, of staying mad at me...
I'd hoped you'd want me to be happy in life, just as you seem to be.
Instead, I'm left with deep, deep scars and I'm totally bereaved.
Some day you will both realize—it was you who rejected me!

I hope you will remember—all the things I did for you before.
You moved away, without a word, and made sure you slammed the door!
For what you were fed were lies and lies and lies and more, galore!
But what is true, and please *REMEMBER*—I'll love you both forevermore!

Life Is All About Love and Loss

Life is all about ups and downs,
Or highs and lows (if you will).
When things go right, they are wonderful;
They enhance the love in our hearts we all feel.

Then there are the losses.
Those are the hardest emotions to bear!
Deep feelings of remorse are so damn hard to process…
When nerves are battered and in need of repair.

Love is much easier to put into words.
Loss is so much more difficult to address.
Love can be euphoric while loss is so upsetting,
And muddled emotions are harder to express!

Love can be heavenly while loss is hell.
Nothing can fill the void of a loss!
As we age, we find out—this is what life is about,
And that nothing is harder than bearing a cross!

If there were no such thing as losses,
We wouldn't know how powerful love can be!
Nothing in life is ever easy but then…
We have to navigate as we go along, accordingly.

DIANNE ROSSOL

Hard Lessons

You learn the hardest lessons from the people you love;
Family shake ups and break ups are the worst!
Even best friends might turn their backs on you,
And annihilate you, as if you are cursed.

Misunderstandings are hard at the best of times.
They can downright hit below the belt—
When you don't have a clue or a reason why...
Those are the worst and the most heartfelt!

You can't totally trust life, though you want to.
For the most part it is incidental and transient.
People come and go as the wind blows...
Like the tides of the sea, there's always movement.

If families can't get along how can the rest of the world?
It's impossible to think of peace on earth!
So much of history has indicated otherwise;
What it would take, is a total rebirth.

The hard lessons that we learn day-to-day
Help pave the way for our journey thereafter.
The growth we accumulate from hard lessons—
Helps develop our attributes and character.

The Creature God Forgot

Some days you feel all alone...
Like you are out there fumbling on your own.
You are in pain like you've never known—
And feel like you are living in the *Twilight Zone*!

You think you're getting nowhere...
All you sense is emotional despair.
You can't figure out how you even got there.
While those around you don't seem to care.

When you think life's plan has been set out for you,
And that you have no voice in what you say or do—
You want someone else to feel your pain too.
You feel like you don't matter and are of no value!

You believe you are the creature God forgot,
And that He isn't giving you a second thought.
You can't believe how hard you have fought.
You are sick and tired of being distraught!

Some days we all feel alone and lonely...
And that life betrays us and just uo only.
Though we know things don't always run smoothly,
It feels like some days, life treats us coldly!

But—out of something bad comes something good.
To be a hundred percent, is an unlikelihood.
Sometimes we all feel alone and misunderstood.
We'd stop our pain and suffering if we could!

DIANNE ROSSOL

We spurt and sputter every now and then,
Before we turn around and bounce back again.
None of us are invincible like supermen!
We are all God's creatures and are only human…

All of us love something, lose something,
And are afraid of something that life may bring:
Healing, grieving, longing, feeling, loving,
Planning, pledging, rushing, yearning…

Think of things in your life that are going well.
Try to step away from that negative spell—
And don't forget life can be heaven as well as hell.
Get your mind off that self-destructive carousel!

No More Cryin' Over You!

It feels just like forever
That I've been cryin' over you!
I think the writing is on the wall—
There is nothing left that I can do!

I've been holding on forever;
I can't even count the years.
I've been ignored and flicked off like a bug.
I've shed way too many tears!

It's time I let you go now!
It's time I close the door!
I've given far too much of my emotional self;
I can't fight that fight anymore!

I feel like I've run out of options...
And I just can't connect with you.
Family or not, it's not meant to be—
We see our lives from a different view!

So with that I say, FAREWELL, stranger!
Safe journey in your future ahead!
I was way too invested in your welfare, and
I'm drowning in the tears I've shed!

Relationships are not one-sided.
I can't turn into someone I'm not!
It's time to worry about my own self-care,
Instead of what was not meant from the start.

DIANNE ROSSOL

Your part in my story is over;
I have nothing left to give!
I need to finally let go of that futile struggle—
I've got my own life to live!

No more of that, I finally get the hint!
I'm giving in to what I'd hoped for...
I could kick myself for caring too much, for too long...
And with that, I'm closing the door!

How Do You Stop the Bleeding?

When you've been shaken to your very core
And the bleeding refuses to stop—
You feel you just can't take anymore;
You just fall on your knees and then drop!

Your last nerve has been ruthlessly triggered,
And it is sucking the life out of you fast.
Just when you are about to surrender—
Because the pain of it is so vast...

There's an inner voice that beckons you
To get up and weather this storm.
It tells you that with a little compression...
The bleeding might stop, and you will transform.

You are more resilient than you think you are!
When you give up and think things can't get worse—
Your emotions have been in a terrible war,
Then something happens and you hit reverse.

You crawl out from that fetal position,
After your survival instincts kick in.
You'll come to the better decision...
Of whether to sink or swim!

This is how the bleeding will stop:
It's the belief that you will overcome.
When you realize, in this fight that you face—
Your inner strength won't let you succumb!

DIANNE ROSSOL

Butterfly Wings

Butterfly wings hold your spirit,
As they flit and float freely to heaven…
While angels escort you to your new home,
They, too, have wings of honoured protection.

Butterflies bless you into your new life,
As they place you at heaven's door.
Then the angels deliver you to God…
And reunite you with loved ones once more.

Butterfly wings signify wholeness…
As you advance to the Promised Land.
You are restored to a healthy new life,
As God takes you by the hand!

Oh, Momma!
(When Naomi Judd Died)

Oh, Momma! Dear Momma! If you only knew—
Just how many people you touched, and truly loved you!
Oh, Momma! If only love could have saved you—
You'd still be here and wouldn't feel so distraught and blue!

I wish you could have known how treasured you were!
You just couldn't find peace, and only God knew the answer.
You were more than worthy; we wish you'd been stronger…
But we are sorry you couldn't hold out any longer.

You couldn't see your place in this world anymore.
Now your soul has entered through heaven's blissful door!
In your mind you were waging a hopeless internal war…
Now you are relieved of turmoil, on that endless shore.

Oh, Momma! Dear Momma! We wish you Godspeed!
And now, with an untroubled mind, you are freed!
You are whole again, robust, and unwearied,
In a place unfettered by mental strife or hypocrisy!

Oh, Momma! May God honour you with His grace!
May His light shine upon your beautiful face!
Though we wish you were still here to love and embrace…
You are at peace and away from that disquieted place!

DIANNE ROSSOL

Thinking of You, Always

The sun that shone upon your life
Will never shine again!
The moon, its glow, you'll never know...
No wind, no clouds, no rain.

You are somewhere now that we don't know,
In a place we all will meet.
A peaceful place of God's intent...
Not yet for us to see.

Who you are—will always be.
We'll forever keep you close.
There's no one like you nor will be.
All we have left is your afterglow.

Our hearts are overflowing...
From all you blessed on us.
We still feel you from afar—
Our love for you is endless!

As You Face Your Mortality

To anyone living with an insidious disease—
May God bless you with strength to fight!
Where there is breath, there is always hope…
May the rest of us stay positive with you, in your light!

As you carry on with resilience and tenacity—
We admire your courage with each passing day.
May you keep fighting with fortitude and persistence!
Determination will take you a long way…

Life is an endurance test, and you have that extra strife,
But with gutsiness and grit you'll go far!
Your spirit will keep you moving forward.
You are already a champion and a star!

Surrendering Control

Right now, we must find a way to surrender—
To circumstances beyond our control.
We need to stay safe and healthy,
During this whole pandemic rigmarole.

We must listen to the scientists,
While going about our lives with caution.
We have to cut back on some privileges (for now),
While life ahead seems so uncertain.

All we can do is hang in, apart, but together,
And stay morally obligated to all.
Some day we will look back and see...
How we managed to dodge this pitfall.

What's important is to stay in contact
With people important to us.
But for now, we must surrender control—
To unfamiliar rules that may seem so strenuous.

Think of those poor souls, who have died,
Amid all this confusion!
For any one of us could be a target...
The vaccine is only part of the solution.

Say a prayer for those who suffer.
Think of what they must be going through.
It will keep you focused on safety...
Of others, and your own family too!

Imagine when this trying time is over,
Get-togethers will be electric!
We will all be able to hug each other again,
Without the fear of becoming sick!

Surrendering control is a hard thing to do,
Especially when others won't comply!
But at least we'll have a clear conscience later,
Even though our patience is in short supply!

Compassion and tolerance are paramount…
In believing we can help in this situation.
The pandemic isn't going away any time soon;
COVID doesn't take a vacation!

Nobody wants to fall victim;
This Devil doesn't discriminate!
As long as we do our part, we lessen our chances—
As we wait for this time in our lives to abate.

DIANNE ROSSOL

The Best Is Yet to Come!

If you think your life is going nowhere,
And you're no longer having any fun...
If you can't feel any lower than you do now,
Know that—THE BEST IS YET TO COME!

You may have hit a rough patch,
And think you might be nearing the end.
You've done everything you can do,
And you can no longer pretend to pretend!

Just wait! Something will surprise you...
And it will come from out of nowhere!
You'll be able to stare down the hopelessness,
That has kept you in so much despair.

The ebbs and flows of life are such,
That the good things outweigh the bad!
Never believe you are alone in this...
Stop using your head as a scratchpad!

Each day as you enter the starting blocks, set to go,
Trying to outrun your misery...
Though you have friends and support for a reason—
Believing THE BEST IS YET TO COME is the key!

PART THREE:
Real Life Stories and Nostalgia

Surprised With Kindness

On a cold December Monday in 1991, I was in line for a coffee at my usual pit stop on the main floor of the office tower where I worked. Not aware of it, I had tears in my eyes and had been trying to hold it together. I was very emotional because it was close to Christmas, and my dad had just died unexpectedly in November. The gal who waited on me asked me what was wrong and why I was so upset. I told her that my dad had suddenly passed away, and I didn't want Christmas to come because that was one of the milestones a person had to go through during the first year for healing and recovery. I told her I dreaded it. She looked at me like she could feel my grief and told me she was sorry and to try and have a good day. I extended a heartfelt thank you for her understanding and went on my way.

My husband and I had been to the cemetery the day before, and the emotions were almost unbearable. This was the first time in my life that I had been shaken to my very core with grief. My dad meant everything to me! While I was waiting for my coffee, I was thinking of the cemetery and how unfair life is. I wasn't sure I could make it through the days ahead.

A couple of weeks prior, I had ordered a wreath for Dad's grave. I had picked it up over the weekend—to be placed on a stand at Dad's grave for Christmas—and had been unable to control myself wondering if I would even be able to go to work.

When I had gone into the flower shop, I burst into uncontrollable tears when the sales lady brought the wreath out to me. This caused the other girls in the flower shop to cry as well. I couldn't hold it together to save my life! The wreath consisted of sprigs of evergreen with little holly berries. It was very plain (yet very symbolic), not to mention fresh and fragrant. I had requested no ribbons or bows. I did not want it to be festive looking. All I wanted was for Dad to know that he would never be forgotten.

Then, on Tuesday, while in the coffee line at work, the same girl (Susan as I found out) handed me a small box wrapped in gold paper with a green ribbon. Inside was a delicate green ceramic bell in the shape of an angel with a gold-trimmed halo. She told me, once again, how sorry she was that Dad had died and hoped that this little angel would offer me a bit of comfort.

That act of goodwill was the kindest gesture a complete stranger had ever blessed on me! It touched me deeply, and I never forgot it. Now the angel sits on display in my curio cabinet. I bring it out at Christmas to sit on my dining room table as a part of my table decorations. From that time on, bells became symbols for both parents, who are now passed. This brought me back to realizing that while there is heartbreak in this life, there is also empathy.

DIANNE ROSSOL

Something Lost, Something Found
(My True Adoption Story)

I'd like to tell you about my being adopted as a newborn, the wonderful life I had, and how at the ripe old age of forty-four, I set out to find my birth mother. After wondering who I looked like and feeling like my adoptive parents and brother were all so good-looking, I needed to find my place and be able to connect with someone who might look like me. I always felt out of place as I was gawky, awkward, and tall and seemingly uncoordinated. Medical history was also a huge part of why I went on this mission. I wanted to know if I might have some devastating hereditary illness I would have the displeasure of experiencing in my future.

Someone from social services (then the government go-between) contacted me within three weeks of my having applied to locate my birth mother. (Nowadays, adoption records are open, and a person can look them up on his or her own without applying anywhere.) As it turned out, my birth mother, Tess (not her real name), had been searching for me for the past thirteen years. The social services representative asked me a bunch of questions. This same person also contacted Tess to see if she had any limitations or boundaries. It was like being interviewed, and it was a long chat. I did have a few reservations and one limitation, which was—I wanted to take this slowly. That rep called me back later, after she spoke with Tess, and suggested that I contact her rather than the other way around. I surmised that it was likely because she had been looking for me a lot longer than I had been looking for her. I certainly did not expect that a connection would happen so fast. I wasn't even sure it would happen at all. It was very overwhelming for a lot of reasons. My emotions were flip-flopping all over the place.

Well, after mustering up the courage, I called her, and my heart was pounding out of my chest. All I could think to say was, "Hi, Tess! What have you been doing for the last forty-four years?" I was afraid that I might be opening a can of worms because I knew nothing about this lady except what the social services rep had passed on. Tess responded by telling me how long she had been searching for me and told me she wanted to come clean to her family. She had been hiding this secret from them, but she had hoped to be able to tell them once we met in person.

My adoptive mom was still alive, and my husband and I were basically her caregivers. She was still living on her own because there was no way she was going into a progressive, assisted living facility. She was living with COPD, which limited what she could and couldn't do. She was becoming weaker and weaker. I explained to Tess that I felt very disloyal to mom for going behind her back and searching her out.

My dad had died in 1991, and I missed him more than I could ever express. I stood helplessly, by his bedside in ICU, and watched him bleed to death from an internal hemorrhage, after begging God and the doctors to save him. Dad was unrecognizable and I could feel him fighting to survive. He was on a ventilator and there were tubes going in and out of him everywhere. There was also blood seeping from every orifice of his body. They could not stop the bleeding because he was on blood thinners. I developed post-traumatic stress disorder (PTSD) and a bereavement disorder that lasted nearly three decades after that fateful night.

Mom and Dad were in their late thirties when I was adopted ("chosen"). Both my husband and I felt Mom would think she hadn't done a good enough job raising me, or some such thing, if I resorted to seeking out my birth mother. We thought it would hurt her deeply.

DIANNE ROSSOL

Mom was very traditional. She (and Dad) did a perfect job raising my brother and me in every way possible! At the time, she was weak and lonely without my dad, and my brother was living on the coast, so my husband and I felt responsible for her and felt the need to be close if she needed us. We only lived twenty minutes from her.

Just a month after speaking with Tess for the first time, we met in the middle of a snowstorm. She and her husband had graciously driven to Calgary to meet me. It coincided with an appointment that she had there with a specialist. It was also very close to Christmas. My husband and I took the day off work, so she and her husband came right to the house rather than meeting at a restaurant, as originally planned. She claimed she didn't know how she was going to react, and I seconded that emotion. I looked just like her and thought I was looking in a mirror, except I was tall, and she was short. She was professing her love for me all these lost years and all I could think about was how much of a stranger she was. The only thing familiar was her looks. We were both standing in my living room dumb-struck. My husband and her husband hit it off immediately, both very down-to-earth.

That first meeting felt awkward as my feelings were a mixed bag. I was terribly nervous and felt like I had done both of my parents a disservice.

Tess was very gracious and came to Calgary to meet me for all future visits. She also made me my favourite chocolate chip cookies. We usually met at a restaurant. The first time we met, she gave me a gold locket with a picture of her in it. Although I was thankful, I had nothing for her except a few pictures of myself and a cup and saucer representing the month she was born. She had done up an album for me of her whole immediate family, including the grandkids she had at the time. I found out I had four half-siblings (one sister and three brothers). That, in itself, was overwhelming. They did not know of me yet.

Over the next three years, we met six times but had written lots of notes and letters to one another in between because she lived in another city. (I still have those cards and letters.) She sent me birthday and Christmas cards and always signed them "love." I could not say those words to her. She was lovely, don't get me wrong! It was just that I loved my mom and dad so much that nothing could top that. My brother (also chosen) came along two years after I did. I was a protective big sister and worshipped the ground he walked on regardless of how different we were.

During the first year of being in touch with Tess, she told me that she had finally let the rest of her family know about me. She also expressed how much of a relief it had been to let go of this deep dark secret. She told me her biggest wish was for me to meet her family by the Christmas of that year. Whoa! Suddenly I was terrified. It was too soon, and I kept thinking about how much my mom would have objected to this. She was still alive, but not in the best of health, and she was on oxygen full time. I could not hurt her like this! I was in an emotional tug-of-war.

Like I said before, I felt disloyal from having had contact with the woman who gave me up for adoption. I did tell Tess that I was very grateful that she did not have a back-alley abortion and instead gave me up, out of love, to a better set of circumstances. I also let her know that I acknowledged that it must have been the hardest decision anyone could make, but I was grateful to her for having made that sacrifice. I also felt sorry for the fact that her own parents disowned her until after I was "gone" and understood how heartbreaking it must have been.

Tess would not tell me who my birth father was, but gave me a few clues, such as his first name (after I pried it out of her) and that he was married, though she did not know it at the time.

He was also ten years older than her. The other revealing bit of information she shared with me was that this man allegedly got a lot of girls into trouble. Tess was sixteen, and I was born when she was seventeen. When she found out she was pregnant, she went to live with her sister until I was born. Her father was very unhappy and would not see her during her pregnancy. She had dropped out of Grade Ten to go to secretarial school to receive her diploma so she could work. It was while she was going to business school that she became pregnant.

I was determined to find out who my birth father was with the tidbits of information she had given me. Apparently, he had threatened to come after her if she told anyone. She was pretty fearful of that. Even after she got married to someone else—during the same year I was born—she still would not reveal my birth father's identity to anyone.

Wanting to find the last piece of the puzzle, I decided to play Sherlock Holmes. One day, while I was at work, I pretended to have an appointment and went over to the business college she had attended to see if they had any scrapbooks I could go through to perhaps find a class picture or something. As luck would have it, I was welcomed to look through what they had in their library. Long story short, I found a newspaper ad that contained pictures of all the teachers who taught at that college the year before I was born. There were two identical ads, so I asked if I could keep one of them. The library staff told me to go ahead, since the glue had worn off, and one copy was lying loosely in the scrapbook. Coincidently, there was a male teacher at the college with the first initial of the name my birth mother had given me of my birth father. I thought nothing of it at the time. I left the college feeling that this mission was a failure, but I thought it had been worth a shot. My intention had initially been to find a class picture with Tess in it. I did not find that picture.

When I first met her, Tess told me the names of my half-siblings and that she had considered naming one of the boys by a different name, but she changed her mind at the last minute. She told me what that name would have been, and I thought it was cool.

I had this good friend Norma whom I worked with, and we had lunch quite often. One day, while we were at lunch, we were just sitting there chatting when out of the blue she handed me a newspaper clipping of an obituary that identified the full name of a man who happened to be that lone male teacher who taught at the business college. What!!! The obituary also gave his age, a description of his life, and that he was married with children. It did not include where he worked, but his vocation fit like a glove. His obituary filled in the missing blanks of the bits and pieces I had initially learned about my birth father. There it was—his first, middle, and last name. His first name was the same name Tess had told me, and his last name was the name she had once thought of naming one of my half-brothers. It was a slam dunk! My impulsive visit to the business school was not for nothing. The clipping of the obituary also gave me a bit of insight as to his medical background, namely the cause of his death and his profession. Plus, Tess had told me he was tall like me. Otherwise, I looked nothing like him. Bingo!

In the meantime, my husband and I had moved, and I did not give Tess our new address. However, having met her was not why we moved. I wanted to put the brakes on for a while, and I did let her know this. She told me she had lots of patience and would wait until I was ready. I was definitely not ready to meet the rest of her family yet although my half-sister Gaye did call me to chat once. I told her, too, that I was not ready to jump in with both feet. I have PTSD and an anxiety disorder, which did not help, although I did not reveal that to her. (I wrote a detailed piece on my struggles with anxiety in my last book *Rhymes for a Reason*.)

Having an anxiety disorder was a detriment in that I was already operating on a last nerve and was fearful of social situations involving a lot of people. I also had a lot of insecurity about what my half-siblings would think about me and had an intense fear of rejection.

I did write Tess one last time to tell her I had put two and two together and found out who I thought my birth father was. I photocopied the newspaper ad I had found at the college and sent it along as well. I did not hear back, of course, because I had not given her my new address, but I knew that she had truly loved this man. That chapter in her life had ended. I did not know her well enough to know if she would have been relieved or sad. My own personal belief is that no matter who it is from a person's past, it is still hard to hear that they have passed away. Memories come flooding back.

We left it there, and unfortunately, my anxiety got the better of me, and I decided to close the door. I kept (and still have) all her genuinely heartfelt letters and pictures, as well as the gold locket with her picture in it. I will remember her as a very down-to-earth soul who cared deeply about her family (and me), and she had a happy and content, generous spirit. At the time, I did not want to share the "sister title" for the sake of Gaye, so she could remain her three brothers' only big sister. (She was the first child to be born, two years after me.)

In 2018, I went on the Internet, on a whim, to see if I could find Tess's name, and I was shocked to find her obituary. She had passed away in 2015. I decided to try and contact Gaye to say how sorry I was, but she did not respond to my call. I'm sure that call, which I left on her answering machine, totally blindsided her, although I did not mention Tess. I just left my name and number. I can certainly understand why Gaye did not respond after all these years. I would like to think she would understand. I was not after anything, but I didn't get a chance to explain. All I wanted to do was express my condolences, albeit three years later.

Although I always wanted to be a part of a Walton's style family with lots of brothers and sisters, this was not meant to be, mostly due to my anxiety and social fears. This is a disability, which is hard to explain to somebody who has never experienced anxiety. For all I know, someone else in that family may be cursed with it too because it can have a genetic component.

I can attest to the fact that not all adoption reunions have happily ever after endings. I mean, it wasn't the worst-case scenario either. It was quite unnerving, to be honest, although the family had been willing to welcome me with open arms. It was not because of my birth mother Tess or my half-sister Gaye that I stopped moving forward with getting to know them. It had a lot to do with the unknowns of what I was getting into. I certainly did have a lot of admiration for both of them, though. Tess was a kind, brave, and giving lady who blessed me with the best life I could have possibly had. I'm also sure it was my loss that I did not wish, at the time, to get to know my half-siblings and their families, as well as other relatives. I'll bet they are a good bunch and are living productive, fulfilling lives. Timing is everything, and it just wasn't the right time. I was grateful, however, that I was able to connect with a bit of my history.

Tess had given me the dates of all my half-siblings' birthdays, and I think of each of them on those days and will always wonder how they are doing and what if…

I truly wish all of them well and hope they are in good health, staying safe, and living the lives they imagined for themselves.

DIANNE ROSSOL

The Sixties

The sixties had such a powerful influence on me as I was very young and impressionable then. Although I was searching for something, it was Woodstock in 1969 that totally mesmerized me. I wrote two poems about Woodstock in my last book, *Rhymes for a Reason*, but still feel there is so much more about the sixties left to express. Those were the years I reminisce about the most.

I believe it was the music that set the tone for that era. A countless number of bands materialized from the British Invasion, iconic bands like the Beatles, the Rolling Stones, the Animals, the Yardbirds, the Kinks, and the Hollies, to name a few. All the British bands were loved and embraced world-wide. The music of the "Flower Power" movement evolved in 1967, with songs such as, "San Francisco" by Scott McKenzie, and Eric Burdon's "San Franciscan Nights" and "Monterey." What about the psychedelic bands, like Jefferson Airplane, the Doors, the Grateful Dead, Janis Joplin, Jimi Hendrix, and Iron Butterfly?! All these bands represented a communal search for universal peace. A lot of the music back then was drug-induced, as was part of the whole Woodstock experience. It was as if the world and its music were acting out with the same cry for peace and unity in some kind of state of hallucination. This musical renaissance (or revival) brought the world together.

There were so many popular genres of music in the sixties and seventies, including Motown, R&B, soul, and pop. I mean, who could resist Smokey Robinson, Lionel Richie and his band the Commodores, Diana Ross, the Temptations, Marvin Gaye, and the Four Tops, as well as countless others? All these bands were like an elixir—great music to soothe your soul and take you somewhere euphoric and familiar. What about Three Dog

Night, the Beach Boys, Led Zeppelin, Creedence Clearwater Revival, and the Doobie Brothers? Oh my gosh! So many bands (all great), each one with a unique sound. Combined, these groups were a cultural celebration. To me, they represented brotherhood, peace, and harmony, and coming together. Then there was Joni Mitchell, a lyrical and vocal genius. She captured the whole Woodstock experience in her free-spirited, philosophical song "Woodstock."

The hippie movement defied convention, (establishment versus anti-establishment), yet it had a universal following. Hippies weren't just incense-burning soul seekers. The movement was more of a peaceful protest for unity. You've probably heard the expression, "If you remember the sixties, you weren't there." If you haven't heard it, the saying refers to the psychedelic drugs that got people high at the many different festivals that went on back then.

Does anyone remember the famous fashion district in London, England, called Carnaby Street, where fashion set the pace of the sixties? It was a time of go-go boots, mini-skirts, bouffant hairstyles, and false eyelashes, followed by long hair, bell-bottoms, peasant blouses, leather vests, tie-dyed T-shirts, love beads, and vintage flowing dresses. Did you know that bell-bottoms are coming back?

Woo-hoo! Even as a senior, I love it!

There were also the duo groups, such as Simon and Garfunkel, the Everly Brothers, and Sonny and Cher! Cher was my idol. She was a raven-haired beauty enhanced by the dresses she wore that were designed by Bob Mackie. If a little girl like me had a dream, it was to look just like Cher. Then there was sexy Elvis with those bedroom eyes...

I was a very timid kid during that time. I was not at Woodstock and have never experienced anything like psychedelic drugs or any drugs at all, for that matter. It was the whole

DIANNE ROSSOL

idea of freedom and serenity that appealed to me. Woodstock seemed like some kind of illusion of love and peace. It wasn't just naked or half-naked bodies and that kind of freedom of expression; it was the whole idea of communal togetherness and that sense of belonging. I was, after all, just a kid and still wet behind the ears. I felt like there was nothing even remotely close to this kind of event that occurred in Canada. How much further ahead the United States seemed culturally. I also felt, at the time, that we were behind in fashion.

Please keep in mind, as you read on, that I'm definitely not a historian, but later in the decade, I do remember some of the following incidents. I was born in Calgary, Alberta, Canada, and was not well versed in current events around the world or of the cultural war going on in the United States. I was still a kid and couldn't fathom just how big the world was yet. I'm not even scratching the surface, but most of the things outlined below are ones I remember, some vaguely, for one reason or another. In the sixties, we only had two channels on TV and no social media.

I don't remember anything monumental that happened in 1960, owing to my age, but I understand that John F. Kennedy (a Democrat) won the American election by defeating Richard Nixon (a Republican). I'm sure my parents told me, but it meant nothing to me at the time. Current events were the farthest thing from my mind, not to mention American politics.

In 1961, McDonald's made its debut, as did the Beatles. Marilyn Monroe died. The IBM Selectric typewriter was introduced. (In the early seventies, I learned to type on a Selectric typewriter.)

In 1962, John Steinbeck won a Nobel Prize for Literature. Harper Lee wrote *To Kill a Mockingbird*. Then there was the Cuban Missile Crisis, which put the world on high alert. All I recall is that air raid sirens went off everywhere, and we were sent running home from school. (In my day, nobody had to be bussed to school because the world was much smaller.) Thank God the Cuban Missile Crisis was averted.

I don't know about you, but I remember that day and I think it was the first time I was ever truly scared. So were my parents. It's hard to forget the piercing sound of the air raid sirens. I think that I started paying more attention to the news of the day after this. That was the day we had to time ourselves on how long it took to get home from school and let the teachers know. I also remember having to cut out current event news articles from the daily newspaper and glue them into scrapbooks.

On November 22, 1963, John F. Kennedy was assassinated—another time we were scared out of our wits. I remember that day quite well and how my brother and I were sent home early from school, before lunch. The world was in shock! We asked Mom if we could stay home the rest of the day. She said no, so back to school we went. (Fast Forward—my husband and I toured Texas in 2019 and were taken to the exact spot in Dallas where John F. Kennedy and his motorcade travelled, and there is an X painted on the roadway where he was shot by Lee Harvey Oswald.) Also, in 1963, Weight Watchers was founded, thank goodness! I'll leave it there.

In 1964, the Toronto Maple Leafs won the Stanley Cup against Detroit (4–3). I mention this because my dad was the practice goalie for the Leafs from 1934 to 1937. He never did, however, get to play in any NHL games. In 1964, the Beatles came to the United States for the first time to be on the Ed Sullivan Show.

In 1965, Sir Winston Churchill died. He was the valiant, successful British prime minister who led Britain through World War II.

In 1966, Indira Gandhi became prime minister of India. She was only the third elected prime minister of India and has been the only lady prime minister since. Walt Disney died in 1966. We all know who the legendary Walt Disney was! I can still hear his voice. Disney classics such as *Bambi, Cinderella, Snow White,* and *Lady and the Tramp* were a huge part of my childhood memories.

In 1967, *Bonnie and Clyde* and *The Graduate* were both hit movies. That year was also labelled "The Summer of Love." The music of the "Flower Power" movement evolved in 1967, as did the onset of "The Age of Aquarius," where people wanted to expand their spiritual consciousness and become one with the earth.

On April 4, 1968, Martin Luther King, civil rights leader, was assassinated in Memphis, Tennessee, by James Earl Ray. (On our Texas tour, we were also taken to the spot where Mr. King stood on a balcony at the Lorraine Hotel and was assassinated. Having had the opportunity to visit the sights where Martin Luther King and John F. Kennedy were murdered brought these times in history to life. Both were very powerfully eye-opening.) John F. Kennedy's brother Bobby Kennedy was also assassinated on June 5, 1968, in California by a man from Jordan named Sirhan. Bobby Kennedy was a presidential candidate at the time. There was also heightened social unrest due to the Vietnam War, which was part of what sparked the "counterculture movement."

In 1969, on August 15, 16, and 17, the famous Woodstock, "An Aquarian Exposition," took place in Bethel New York, on Max Yasgur's dairy farm. As I mentioned before, it felt like a fantasy to me. Consequently, I became obsessed with it. Two hundred thousand people were expected to show up for a weekend of peace and music. Instead, nearly half a million came—most looking for a new direction—while others protested the Vietnam War in other cities in America. Also significant was that in 1969, the Beatles recorded their final album together, *Abbey Road*. The movie *Butch Cassidy and the Sundance Kid* was released in theatres.

On July 16, 1969, the Apollo 11 Saturn V rocket landed on the moon. "That's one small step for man, one giant leap for mankind," were astronaut Neil Armstrong's legendary words. He was the very first man to walk on the moon, along with astronaut Buzz Aldrin. An American flag was planted there. This was a legendary and historic moment in history. (My husband and I were fortunate to be able to visit NASA in Houston during the fiftieth anniversary of this mission, while we were on a tour of Texas. We were able to see the mission control room, which was reconstructed as an exact replica of the one that was monitoring that mission in 1969. The Saturn V rocket, now out of commission, is being housed there in a building all on its own. The enormities of the boosters on that rocket were out of this world—no pun intended. The tour of that facility was nothing short of mind-blowing and a must-see in Houston.)

The sixties had a huge influence on my taste in music, more than anything. It also created an awareness of how big the world was, and that racial bias is real, unfortunately. The Vietnam War went on for so long that there were protests right through the sixties to 1975, when the war ended.

As the American rock band the Young Bloods inspired us with the lyrics in their song "Get Together," plus the insight and vision in John Lennon's song "Imagine," I feel we need these songs to "re-evolve" as universal theme songs. Lyrics to both these songs are nothing short of brilliant and are also relevant to what is desperately needed in our world today.

We are supposed to be our Brothers' Keepers, after all.

DIANNE ROSSOL

A Story of Resilience and Inspiration

A girl I grew up with, who was a good friend for forty-six years and whom I will refer to as Janet (Jan), was in a very serious car accident when she was twenty-four years old. This happened in 1975. She was a passenger in a car that hit a pothole on a back-country road and the car toppled, end over end, into a ditch. Jan was not wearing a seatbelt at the time. Seatbelts were not mandatory in the early seventies, unfortunately (but also fortunately, as I will explain). As the car hit the pothole, Jan somehow got jolted out of the open passenger window and landed on her neck in a ditch away from the vehicle. She lay there, unable to move, and went in and out of consciousness. Her boyfriend, who was the driver, sustained a broken shoulder on impact.

It took an ambulance a while to get there owing to this pothole was on a country back road in Alberta. Keep in mind, there were no cell phones then either. They would have had to depend on a passerby for help. Jan was transported to the hospital in critical condition.

The car had rolled, and the entire passenger side of the car was mashed flat into the seat. If she had been wearing a seatbelt, she would have died on impact. This is the only instance I have heard of where it was better NOT to have been buckled into a seatbelt.

Jan was in critical condition for about a month. Doctors put one of those cage contraptions (it's actually called a halo) around her head, which was fastened with bolts bored into her skull to stabilize her neck. Her spine had been severed at the neck. The doctors told her she would never walk again and that she was paralyzed from the neck down. In other words—she was a quadriplegic. At the time, they also told her that her long-term prognosis was not favourable and that people with this severe of an injury only live a few years, if that.

Jan spent a very long time in the hospital (about six months) and then was transferred to rehabilitation to learn how to cope with the "death of her own body," as she put it. From then on, she alluded to any part of her body as THE hand or THE foot or THE… for any other body part. She had to disassociate herself from her body as part of accepting her circumstances. This was one way of dealing with her situation.

Jan's boyfriend/fiancé, at the time, came to the hospital to visit her, but after he found out that she was permanently paralyzed, he disappeared from the scene.

Jan received a settlement from the municipal district in charge of where this pothole was located in the road. She either had the choice of taking a lump sum or a certain non-taxable amount of money per month, adjusted for the cost of living, for as long as she lived. She chose the latter. Once again, this was a very fortunate choice because up until I lost touch with her in 2009, when she was fifty-eight years old, she was collecting a reasonably handsome sum of money each month that she did not have to pay taxes on. The best part is that she was still alive, to the disbelief of doctors. This settlement money helped her with any medical expenses incurred, such as catheters, homecare, and the maintenance of an electric wheelchair. She was also able to install an elevator in her home.

It was through a lot of counselling and inner strength that she got to the acceptance phase of her accident. We had been very good friends since we were teenagers, when every Sunday night she would come to my family home for a roast beef dinner, which was customary. She was like a sister for a lot of our growing up years. We were also roommates in our early working years before her accident.

After her accident, when I would go and visit her in the hospital, Jan would ask me what I had been doing. I was playing baseball, bowling, and was active in other activities that she and I would normally have done together, but I was afraid to say anything because of her situation. It was heartbreaking to see her this way and I, too, was having a hard time accepting her prognosis. She totally picked up on the fact that I was mum about what I had been doing to spare her feelings, and she gave me a rather stern talking to. She told me that she had accepted her situation and that I should too! She wanted me to be myself around her and not walk on eggshells. After that, I told her everything. She wanted to be treated like a normal person with normal abilities. I so admired her for being able to deal with the cards she had been dealt.

After she had been rehabilitated, Jan initially ended up in a group home for paralyzed people, a lot of them around her age. The facility had common areas, like a kitchen and living room. Each person had their own private room (more like a suite) where they were allowed to have their personal furnishings with them. The residents were well looked after in this facility, and each of them had similar outcomes from debilitating accidents. It is important for people facing situations like this to know they are not the only ones living with the same circumstances.

Immediately after the accident, while in the hospital, Jan had her own room, but she was later moved into a room with a fellow who had broken his neck by diving off a rock into a pond. He had also become a quadriplegic. He, too, was critical at first, but he and Jan had become good friends with similar needs and similar injuries. Both ended up in the same group home.

In time, Jan learned to use a hand brace which had a slot in it so that she could insert a fork handle. She was able to feed herself with limited hand-to-mouth movement, though her hands were gnarled, and she could not use her fingers. She was fortunate to have this hand-to-mouth ability, albeit limited.

Eventually, Jan got a job whereby she was transported, via

a Handibus, to her place of work at a busy bank in downtown Calgary. There, she was a receptionist who worked the phones. She pushed the switchboard buttons with the rubber end of a pencil inserted into her hand brace. She developed a very keen memory and aced that job with ability and confidence. She had memorized the extensions of each and every employee and there were upwards of seventy-five (if I remember correctly). She was able to sign for things that arrived by messenger, as well, with a little manoeuvring. She was there for three years.

Jan decided to go to college where she learned the art of interior design. She took her exams verbally. She aced those courses as well. While at the college, she met a man from South America, Carlos, to whom she taught some English after they had developed a friendship. He was attending the college, but I can't remember what courses he was taking. He did have an engineering background before he immigrated to Canada. He could also speak English enough to understand what was being taught. The association with Jan led to more than a friendship, and Carlos proposed to her. He was an able-bodied, very ambitious, kind man who was willing to sacrifice many things to marry her. He was very cultured and loved the opera, and both loved horses, music, and good movies.

Carlos taught Jan to speak Spanish, and she also went to school to take proper Spanish lessons. She became fluent in Spanish, and Carlos became fluent in English. (I only hope Jan writes an inspirational book about her life someday because she had had a very a difficult life even before her accident. Meeting Carlos was a dream come true and a life-changer for her.)

As I mentioned before, I haven't heard from Jan since 2009, but so far as I know they are still going strong and are living in South America. They have been married now for nearly forty years. I was her maid of honour at their wedding and my dad was master of ceremonies. Dad was also instrumental in helping Jan secure her first motorized wheelchair through the Shriners organization. Their home was impeccably designed and decorated like a show home in Calgary, and I expect their home in Chile is too.

Jan faced her challenges with fortitude and resolve, and she taught me a lot about resilience and the ability to overcome obstacles, no matter how big or small they seem. She also taught me that the human spirit is stronger than we give it credit for and that we can do anything we set our minds to, limits or no limits. If there is an opportunity, don't be afraid to take it!

I will always fondly remember and admire Jan and her self-less and kind husband. She bravely made the sacrifice to move to South America for Carlos as this is his homeland, and he has family there. Before we lost touch, they had spoken of moving there often, once Carlos retired. Besides, the temperatures there are moderate year-round, which is very good for Jan's health.

I do hope both of them are still living and remain happy and healthy.

PART FOUR:
A Camping Adventure

The Adventures of Fuzzy, Dusty, Leaky, Picky, and Kate (The Cabin)

Fuzzy, Dusty, Leaky, and Picky
Were friends who did everything together!
They were of the good guy variety, most of the time
And swore they'd be best friends forever!

Picky had an easy-going girlfriend, Kate…
All the guys loved her personality.
She knew how to razz them and tell good jokes,
And, of course, none of them took it personally.

Now Fuzzy, Dusty, and Leaky planned a camping trip.
They spent most of their weekends outdoors.
They loved campfires, hot dogs, and pan-fried fish,
But once in a while they'd get caught in a downpour!

They were all packed up and ready to go;
Their pickup was full to the limit.
They hadn't heard the latest forecast, so didn't know—
They'd need their truck and everything in it!

Dusty remembered to pack his camera.
Fuzzy brought his arctic sleeping bag.
Leaky didn't forget his gumboots this time;
If his boots were to leak (as usual) it would be a drag!

Picky and Kate wanted to join them, just for the day.
The boys chose a place near Shady Pines.
It happened to be a bit off the beaten track—
In the backwoods where the dirt road winds.

Though Picky's old truck had a canopy on it,
His friends brought a rather large tent.
None of them were prepared very well—
For any nasty, unexpected, weather event!

All the boys brought camping equipment,
And a plastic tarp for the tent just in case—
In this instance, their large tent came in handy,
Because they were going to need lots of space!

It took them a while, but they made it;
They set up camp and lit a roaring fire.
Kate and Picky decided to stay the night...
Though they didn't know what was to transpire!

They guzzled some beer and ate hot dogs.
The winds started to howl through the trees!
The weather was about to turn, so they thought
They'd better douse the fire with water from the creek.

They knew from experience it was going to rain!
The air was feeling humid and damp.
They installed the tarp across the top of the tent;
This is a trick they learned at kid's camp.

All five of them piled into the spacious tent—
With their sleeping bags and mattresses in place!
Kate was unusually quiet being in a tent with four guys;
She hadn't brought her pillow or her makeup case.

DIANNE ROSSOL

"You don't need makeup anyhow!" declared Picky.
"For Pete's sake—you are out in the woods!
I'll blow up the air mattress pillow for you...
And then everything should be good."

With the snoring, the owl hoots, and cricket chirps—
They managed to catch a few zees...
Then there was a lightning bolt and crack of thunder!
The winds started to swirl in a frenzied breeze!

As Murphy's Law would have it, it poured like hell—
To where they thought the tent would wash away.
At least the tent had a floor and there were no holes,
But the ferocious weather made it hard to stay!

"So much for fishing tomorrow!" Leaky exclaimed.
"If this continues, we'll have to head for home.
We can't build a campfire in this deluge,
And we will get soaked right through to the bone."

They decided to pack up and head for home,
And try to get out while they still could.
It was 1:00 a.m. and there was already plenty of mud,
And their firewood was soaked, but good!

They had to make their escape early,
Before the mud swallowed the tires of their trucks!
It was blustery and pouring rain quite hard—
But sand and kitty litter would keep them unstuck.

Dusty wouldn't get his nature photographs this time,
And Fuzzy wouldn't get to stretch out in the sun.
They wouldn't catch any fish for breakfast.
Being rained out wasn't that much fun!

They spotted a dimly lit cabin just off the road—
And wondered if they should make the stop.
The consensus was to quickly check things out.
A weathervane was spinning wildly on the rooftop!

Rain was teeming down from all directions.
The sky was pitch-black amid the torrent!
Trees were rustling with intensity;
The winds were gusting, and it was so violent!

Of course, there was no cell service,
So they couldn't contact anyone—
Though friends knew generally where they were,
Despite the change in weather, all of a sudden!

Dusty knocked on the cabin door—
There was no one inside, as it turned out.
It was unlocked so he reluctantly went in…
Then from the doorway he heard a demanding shout!

"WHO ARE YOU? WHAT DO YOU WANT?"
a voice bellowed.
Dusty turned around as calmly as he could…
"Is everything alright, are you trapped up here?"
Trying not to sound misunderstood.

DIANNE ROSSOL

"We didn't see a vehicle, so we stopped to check—
Do you need any help in this wicked storm?
We are on our way back home and saw your light
And know you can't access a phone!"

Dusty introduced himself as Carl O'Grady.
That was his real name!
"Are you Cameron O'Grady's son?" asked the stranger.
"He owns the hardware store on fourth and Main."

"Yes, that's me, and who are you?" Dusty asked.
"Why don't you have a vehicle up here?
We stopped to make sure you weren't stranded
But if you're okay, we'll just disappear."

"I'm Jake, an old friend of your dad.
My wife brought me up here for the weekend.
She went to visit her sister in Vancouver;
This gave me some quiet fishing time to spend.

"Why don't you and your friends bunk here tonight?
So you're not out in the wind and the storm!
I'll light a fire so you can dry out all cozy-like…
At least tonight you'll be safe and warm."

Dusty dashed out to let the rest know;
All were delighted to be asked inside.
They grabbed their stuff and ran to the door;
This would beat the heck out of a rough joyride.

Dusty (Carl) introduced Jake to the others:
Kate, Fuzzy (Grant), Picky (Hal), and Leaky (Paul)…
They were thankful for the invitation
And didn't really want to be driving in that squall!

"We appreciate the offer; thanks so much!" Kate said.
They were grateful for not having to drive!
The roads were just like a mucky slough—
Though they knew they'd somehow survive.

There were hot toddies all around,
And they chatted for an hour or so.
As they called it a night, and tried to get some sleep,
They could hear the fierce wind blow!

"How did you get your nicknames?" Jake wondered.
"Well," Dusty replied, "my passion is to take photos…
So my friends called me *Dusty Lenscap* and it stuck.
I'd like to be a wildlife photographer, I suppose!"

Jake then turned to Fuzzy, "How about you?"
"I always wanted to become a cop;
I have a keen interest in detective movies
And I'm trying to solve mysteries non-stop."

Leaky chimed in, "Well, I guess I'm next!
I got the nickname *Leaky Gumboots* when I was a boy.
I used to jump into any mud puddle I could find…
And to this day, it's something I still enjoy!"

DIANNE ROSSOL

Picky piped up, "I'm particular about certain things,
I guess I have a bit of an obsession...
My clothes had to match when I was a kid;
I'm still rather *picky* in others' opinion."

There was a loud bang on the storage shed—
That sent them into high alert!
A pine tree had come crashing down,
But thank goodness nobody was hurt!

Jake took off outside to take inventory...
And make sure it was safe to be inside.
No sign of any more trees falling...
But a black bear was lurking about, preoccupied.

The bear had been nestled up in the tree,
Before it toppled onto the woodshed!
The falling tree jolted the bear off, with a walloping thump
It seemed shaken up but wasn't dead.

Jake watched it for a few minutes...
To make sure it wasn't injured too badly.
He would have to get a hold of a park ranger,
To remove this nomad, unfortunately!

He would check again in the morning
To see if this stranger was gone.
The kids were all snug in their sleeping bags.
They'd check out the damages at dawn.

The weather was much calmer by morning.
The rain had stopped, and the wind had died down.
They enjoyed a breakfast of ham and eggs,
Before they were to head back to town!

Leaky said, "Let's go out and survey the damage;
We'll see if the bear is still lurking about.
We can all pitch in and cut the tree into pieces,
And fix the woodshed and the cabin's downspout.

"Jake, you've been so gracious in letting us stay here…
That's the least we could do for you!
We had hoped to stay out for the weekend anyways,
So, we will see what we can do."

The bear was disoriented and panting profusely!
They knew it had sustained some kind of trauma.
With cell service restored, Jake called the forest ranger.
It was a larger cub—but where was its momma?

The bear was sedated and then removed,
And taken for treatment at a wildlife sanctuary…
They hoped it would end up alright,
And that it wasn't too serious of an injury!

The kids stayed the morning to clear up the debris;
Kate straightened up things in the cabin.
Jake welcomed them to stay another night.
They agreed without hesitation.

DIANNE ROSSOL

They went fishing later that afternoon,
So trout and walleye were on their dinner agenda…
So were some baked spuds and beans,
And maybe a wee dram of vodka!

It just so happened, momma bear showed up
With another cub in tow.
The pair was wandering around the cabin—
All anyone could say was, "OH NO!"

They sat in their trucks and waited a while,
Hoping the rain had washed the injured cub's scent away.
The mother hadn't tried breaking into the cabin,
But Jake did say he had some bear spray.

If the bears smelled their catch, they'd linger…
Or the mother could even become aggressive!
So they drove away and called the park ranger back.
They didn't want to be held captive!

The wildlife people would remove the bears;
Then release them a few miles from there.
Then later, after the other cub was rehabilitated—
They'd reunite it with the pair.

They returned to the cabin after waiting an hour,
While the wildlife people captured the bears.
The ranger called Jake back to say it was safe
For them to return without a care!

They feasted on their fish as planned.
What an exciting weekend it had been!
This would not be the last time they'd be together
They couldn't wait to get together again!

Jake really enjoyed the kids' company.
He heard back again from the forest ranger.
The injured bear's shoulder had been dislocated,
But he'd be okay; he's a lucky creature!

Things don't always go as planned, BUT
Their adventure turned out to be great one!
They caught some fish and had lots of tales to tell...
It was more fun than they could have imagined.

Jake let his wife know not to pick him up—
He'd get a ride home with his new-found friends.
They all thanked Jake for his kind hospitality!
It had been one of their best ever camping weekends!

DIANNE ROSSOL

CPSIA information can be obtained
at www.ICGtesting.com
Printed in the USA
BVHW072344180123
656578BV00001B/98

9 781039 166424